Singing Strings

Written and Illustrated by Larry Kettelkamp

WILLIAM MORROW & COMPANY 1958

Grateful recognition is given to Professor George Hunter, School of Music, University of Illinois, Urbana, Illinois, for his helpful suggestions.

Published simultaneously in the Dominion of Canada by George J. McLeod Limited, Toronto.

Printed in the United States of America.

Library of Congress Catalog Card No. 58-8001

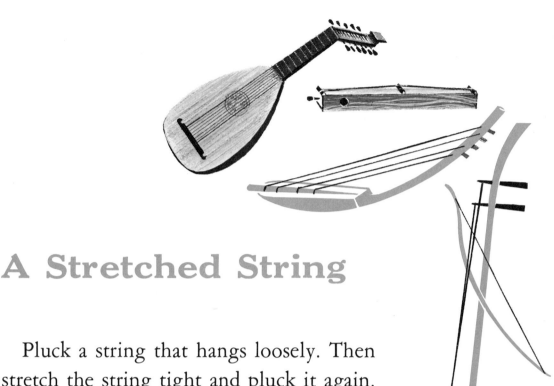

A Stretched String

Pluck a string that hangs loosely. Then stretch the string tight and pluck it again. You will hear a sound the second time only. This simple fact was learned from the hunter's bow. It is the principle behind all stringed musical instruments.

The instruments pictured on this page are some of the first ever invented and some of the most important. They have led to the development of the stringed instruments we use today. These early

3

Materials

instruments are so simple that you can build instruments like them with materials that cost less than a dollar or that are already in your home.

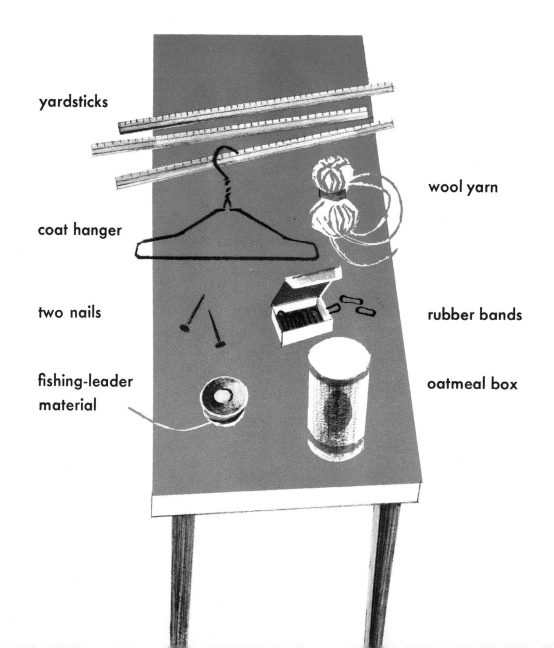

yardsticks

coat hanger

wool yarn

two nails

rubber bands

fishing-leader material

oatmeal box

Here are the music-making materials you will need to gather:

Three wooden yardsticks
Two yards of wool yarn
A coat hanger
Two nails about an inch long
Rubber bands (size number 8)
One round oatmeal box
Fishing-leader material (This nylon line can be bought at either a hardware store or a sporting-goods store. A roll of twenty-pound line will cost only a few cents.)

You will also need these tools: a pair of pliers, a hammer, a coping saw, a jack-knife, and a pair of scissors.

With these materials and tools you can make some of the same musical instruments that were made hundreds or even thousands of years ago. The instruments you build will help you learn how stringed instruments came to be and how they are played.

Tools

5

Singing Bowstrings

More than 10,000 years ago men made and used the bow and arrow to hunt wild animals. A strong, tightly strung bowstring hummed when the arrow was released. The humming sound probably pleased the ear of the hunter, for he knew it meant that the bow was strung correctly. Some of these early men became interested in the clear sound of the bowstring. An arrow was not needed to make this sound; the magic tone was in the string itself. A tightly strung bowstring produced a high tone; a loosely strung string made a lower tone. A thick string made a lower tone than a thin string of the same length on the same bow. These men must have made many experiments to solve the puzzles of the singing bow-string.

Finally someone thought of adding another shorter bowstring behind the first. Now more than one tone could be played on the same bow, since the shorter string would sound a higher note than the first, if it was stretched equally tight. It may have been in this way that the hunter's bow became the harp, the first musical instrument to use stretched strings.

When the bowstring harp was popular

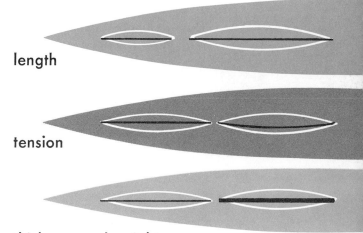

length

In each example the string on the left sounds a higher pitch than the string on the right.

tension

thickness and weight

in Egypt, about 3000 years ago, men had already strengthened the sound of the instrument. Some harps were made so that the lower end of the bow widened into a sounding board. On others the end of the bow was made into a sounding box covered with parchment. All of the Egyptian harps were open like the hunter's bow, and the strings were the only connection between the upper and lower parts of the bow.

The Egyptians used harps of many sizes. A small harp was strapped to a player's shoulder, so that he could move about as he played. Larger harps rested on stands or on the ground.

The Egyptians left many drawings of these harps in their picture writing. Harps

vertical harp

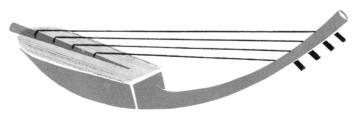

shoulder harp

have also been found in some tombs of ancient Egyptian kings. The very dry climate helped to preserve them. One harp was found with the strings still stretched, and it still could be played, even though it had been silent in a tomb for about 3000 years.

The harp was improved by inserting a rod between the ends of the wooden bow, making it stronger. Now the curved bow did not take all the pull of the strings. This type of pillar harp became the national instrument of Ireland. There the harp was given the name we use, which means to pluck.

9

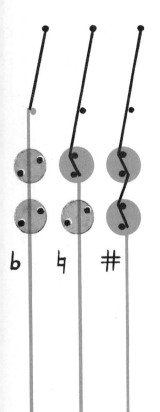

Positions of the gripper hooks match those of the pedals on Page 11.

b   ♮   #

Before the hunter's bow became a harp, men had already made strings of many materials. Woven animal hair and vegetable fibers were used. Later it was found that fine strings could be made of gut from the intestines of animals. When the supporting post was finally added to the harp, the stronger frame made it possible to use wire strings.

Early pillar harps were usually tuned to simple scales, such as the scale sounded by the white keys of a piano. As music became more complicated, more in-between notes, called half steps, were used. Soon harps were needed on which all of the whole steps and half steps could be played quickly and easily. Some people built harps with extra strings for the extra notes. Others thought the problem could be solved by making each string play more than one note.

About 140 years ago in Paris, Sebastian

10

Erard made a set of foot pedals for the harp. These pedals moved rods that were hidden inside the front pillar and were connected to gripper hooks at the upper end of each string. By raising or lowering a pedal a group of strings were raised or lowered one half step. This could be done quickly, and the hands of the harpist were free to continue playing on the strings.

This amazing harp could be played in any key. It had forty-seven strings, giving it a broad range of tones. It is the type of harp used today as a solo instrument or as a part of a modern orchestra. The next time you see or hear a harp being played, think of the hunter's bow with its single string and of the many changes it went through before it became the modern harp.

When the pedal is in the middle position the string's note is natural (♮). In the raised position the string is longer, lowering its note ½ step (♭). In the lowered position the string is shorter, raising it ½ step (#).

♭ ♮ #

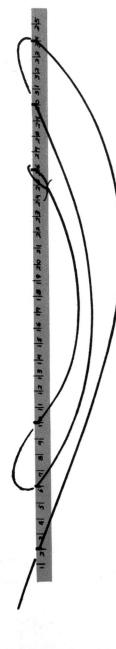

Building a Bowstring Harp

To build a simple harp you will need a wooden yardstick, a coping saw, and a roll of 20-pound nylon leader line. Saw slots about ¼ inch deep at the markings for 2, 6, 10, 26, 30, and 34 inches. Slip the end of the nylon line into the slot at the 26-inch mark and tie the line around the yardstick. Next run the line through the slot at the 10-inch mark and then through the slot at the 6-inch mark, as shown in the drawing. Run the line through the 30- and 34-inch marks at the opposite end of the stick and back through the 2-inch mark. Cut the line, leaving a few extra inches for tying it off.

Rest the 36-inch end of the yardstick on the floor and bow the stick into a gentle curve. Pull the line through all of the slots, so that it is tight while the stick is held in a bowed position. Tie the free end of the line through the slot and around the stick at the 2-inch mark, still keeping the yardstick bent in the bow shape.

If you pull a little on one string, you will loosen it and tighten one or both of the other strings. By pulling, plucking the strings, and listening, you can tune the three strings to a pleasing chord. If you know the sounds of the sol-fa syllables, do-re-mi-fa-sol-la-ti-do, try tuning the strings to do-mi-sol or do-fa-la.

To make the strings produce a louder sound, press part of the yardstick bow firmly against a table top. Vibrations from the strings will pass through the bow to the table. You will then hear the sound vibrations from the strings, bow, and table combined, and the sound will be much stronger. Try holding the bow against a door, a cabinet, or a wall and see how much different materials amplify the sound of the strings.

Keyboard Stringed Instruments

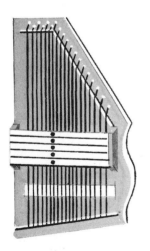

dulcimer

Autoharp

Before the Keyboard

While the strings of the harp ran perpendicular to the sound box, other instruments had strings that ran across a sound box. Two of the oldest of these instruments were the psaltery and the dulcimer, which were alike except for the way they were played. Both were made with wire or gut strings stretched across a sounding box. The psaltery was played by plucking the strings with the fingers or a pick, while the strings of the dulcimer were struck with hammers. The modern zither and Autoharp are variations of the ancient psaltery, and the dulcimer is used today in gypsy bands. Ideas taken from the psaltery and dulcimer were used in the development of the keyboard stringed instruments.

14

Building a Monochord

About 2500 years ago a Greek mathematician named Pythagoras made important experiments with a simple one-stringed instrument called a monochord. *Mono* means one and *chord* means string.

To build a monochord, you will need the 20-pound nylon leader line, a yardstick, a board at least ½ inch thick and a little longer than the yardstick, and 2 nails.

Place the yardstick on the board and, with the hammer, drive the nails partly into the board next to the ends of the yardstick. The nails should be exactly 36 inches apart. With a pair of pliers bend the nails slightly toward each other. Cut off a length of the nylon line and tie each end to the head of one of the nails so that the line runs straight between them. Slide each knot down to the base of the nail to which it is tied. Straighten the nails with

15

monochord

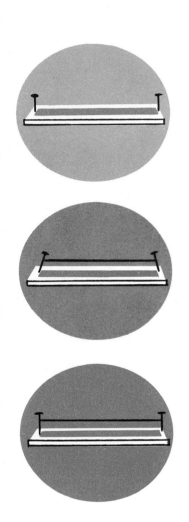

the pliers. Then slide the knots back up the nails so that the line is about ½ inch above the board.

Saw off a 2-inch section of the yardstick at the 34-inch mark. Replace the yardstick on the board under the string, so that the zero end touches one nail. If you have tied the string and bent the nails correctly, the string should now be tight enough to make a clear tone. If you rest the monochord on a table top, the table will help to amplify the sound.

Pluck the string and listen to it. Now stand the 2-inch section of yardstick on edge along the 18-inch mark, so that it forms a bridge over which the string passes. Pluck each half of the string; the two halves will sound alike and each half

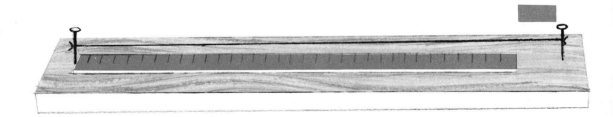

will make a tone one octave higher than the tone the original open string made. Take the bridge away and sing *do* on the pitch of the open string. Continue singing re-mi-fa-sol-la-ti-do. The last note you reach will be the same as the sound of each half string when the bridge is at the 18-inch mark.

Now slide the bridge to the 9-inch mark, making the longer section of string three times the length of the shorter section. The tones they make are those of *do* in one octave and *sol* in the next.

Pythagoras worked out these mathematical relationships on the monochord, and his experiments helped to explain the music of the stretched string that had been used for thousands of years.

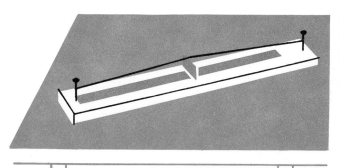
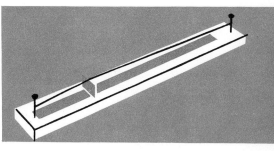

Drop a handkerchief over the nylon string near one nail. Holding the handle of a table knife, strike the string with the sharp edge of the blade. Hold the blade on the string after you have struck it. The knife blade makes the string vibrate and at the same time forms a bridge over which the string passes. Try striking the string at different places with the blade, always holding the blade against the string after you have struck it. Because the handkerchief damps the vibrations at one end of the string, only the part between the blade and nail at the other end vibrates. Since the blade acts as a movable bridge, shortening or lengthening the vibrating part of the string, you can play a tune by shifting the position of the knife each time you strike the string.

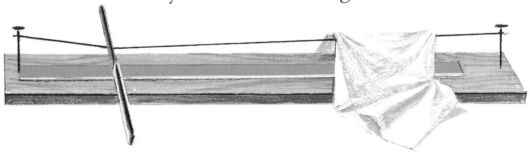

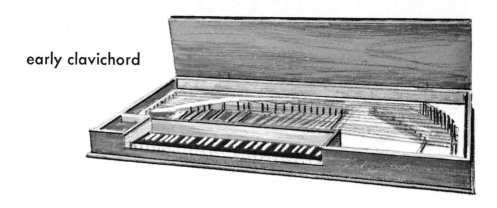

early clavichord

Three Keyboard Instruments

A movable bridge striking a string was the principal behind the first keyboard stringed instrument, the clavichord. *Clavi* means key and *chord* means string. The clavichord came from the dulcimer, for the strings of both instruments were struck. The new instrument also looked something like a dulcimer with a keyboard added. Each key ended in a metal tangent just beneath one of the strings. When a key was struck the tangent flew up, striking the string and forming a bridge, just as the table knife formed a bridge in the monochord experiment. The vibrations of

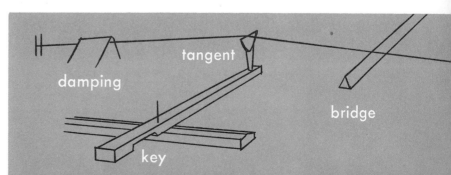

clavichord
mechanism

damping   tangent

bridge

key

the string were damped near one end by a felt cloth placed on one side of the bridge made by the tangent. The clavichord could be played louder or softer by striking the keys sharply or gently.

In the hands of a skilled musician the instrument became very expressive. The sound of a clavichord was gentle, even softer than that of a guitar. Early clavichords were not expensive and became popular in many homes. Often the instruments were so small that they could be carried under an arm from place to place.

Then a stronger-toned mechanical stringed instrument was also developed. Its strings were plucked, like those of a harp, instead of being struck. The new instrument was called a harpsichord. It came from the psaltery.

When one of its keys was pushed down, a narrow piece of wood called a jack was pushed up beside a string. A small prong of leather or a quill point was fastened to a tongue in the wooden jack. As the jack passed by the string, the plectrum, as the quill or leather prong was called, plucked the string just as a finger plucks a harp string.

The harpsichord sounded louder than the clavichord and could be used with groups of instruments, but its strings could not be made to sound louder or softer by changing the pressure on the keys. As a result, the harpsichord had an even sounding tone. Composers of the

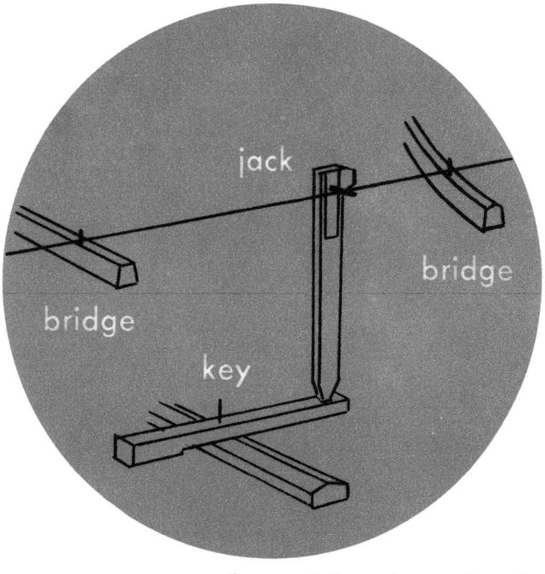

harpsichord

harpsichord mechanism

```
c4
b3
a3
g3
f3
e3
d3
c3
b2
a2
g2
f2
e2
d2
c2
b1
a1
g1
f1
e1
d1
c1
b
a
g
f
e
d
middle C
B1
A1
G1
F1
E1
D1
C1
B2
A2
G2
F2
E2
D2
C2
B3
A3
G3
F3
E3
D3
C3
B4
A4
```

notes of the piano keyboard

time, such as Handel, Scarlatti, and J. S. Bach, wrote music especially for it. Today this music sounds better if it is played on the instrument for which it was originally written, the harpsichord.

The harpsichord was the most popular keyboard stringed instrument for several hundred years. But many people had not forgotten that the weaker-sounding clavichord could be played more expressively. They wanted an instrument with the power of the harpsichord and the controlled volume of the clavichord. They began to think that an instrument like this would have to be one in which strings were struck instead of plucked.

In 1709 Bartolommeo Cristofori developed a striking mechanism, which he fitted to a harpsichord. The action in his device consisted of covered hammers, which fell back quickly after striking the strings, so that the sound was clear, much

22

When the key is pressed, the hammer bounces against the string and the damper is raised to let the string vibrate.

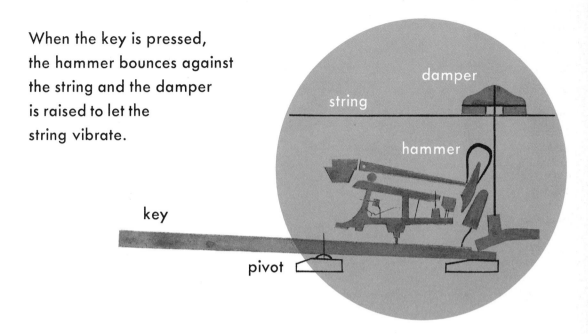

piano
mechanism

as the hand hammers were used on the dulcimers. A strong pressure on a key produced a louder sound than a gentle pressure, so Cristofori called his instrument a pianoforte, which meant soft-loud. Although it has been improved, Cristofori's basic principle of action is still used today. However, many other changes were also introduced before the piano was developed as we know it today.

Early pianos had a framework of wood to support the strings. Later, iron was used, and finally the iron frame was cast in a single unit. Early strings were not thick and were made of steel or brass. Today strings are made of heavier cold-drawn steel. The cast-iron frame of the piano of

spinet

concert grand

today supports a pull of around seventeen tons. Its volume can easily fill an entire concert hall with sound.

The largest pianos are the grand pianos. Smaller grands, often called baby grands, are also made. About 150 years ago the upright piano was developed and soon became popular. The frame of the upright piano is tipped, so that the strings run up and down instead of horizontally. The smallest upright is called a spinet. It is very popular today. The sound of a spinet is amazingly loud in relation to its size.

Today the piano has a place in the musical world like that of the lute 300 years ago. It is both a solo instrument and an accompanying instrument. It is a good instrument for beginning musicians, but it is so expressive that many musicians spend a lifetime trying to develop all its possibilities. Often the piano has been called the king of the instruments.

upright piano

25

The Guitar Family

Like harps, the instruments in the guitar family are plucked. Each harp string sounds a single note, but in the guitar family each string can sound many notes. The strings on these instruments pass across a sounding box, along a special type of neck, and are attached to tuning pins in a peg box. The neck has many small cross bridges, called frets, added to it. If a string is pressed against the neck just above a fret, the fret becomes a tiny bridge over which the string must pass. According to the position of the fret on the neck, the string is made shorter or longer and the pitch of the string is raised or lowered. In this way many notes can be played with a small number of strings.

The lute was one of the earliest and most important plucked stringed instruments with a neck. Beginning in the elev-

Frets of the guitar
are of metal.

26

enth and twelfth centuries the lute was popular in Europe for about 600 years. Lutes came to Europe from the Orient. The name comes from the Arabic word *al-ud,* which means wood. When spoken fast, the Arabic name sounds like lute. European lutes were made of very light wood and came in many sizes.

The lute had a large, pear-shaped sound box with a rounded back. Its sound opening was in the form of a delicately carved, perforated opening. The strings were anchored at a bridge glued to the face of the sound box and ran along the neck to the peg box. The peg box was bent at almost a ninety-degree angle to the neck to help keep the light instrument in balance. Lutes had frets made of gut string tied around the neck.

Lutes usually had six strings. Sometimes the strings were doubled to give more sound, but the highest string was al-

Frets of the lute are of gut tied around the neck.

ways a single one. Sometimes the double strings were tuned in unison, sometimes in octaves.

At the time of its greatest popularity the lute was to its musical world what the piano is to ours today. It was used for accompaniment, for solos, and in instrumental groups. Almost every composer wrote for the lute, and anyone who studied music seriously learned to play it.

An instrument much like the lute is the guitar. The six strings of the guitar are tuned to the notes: E^2, A^2, D^1, G^1, B^1, and e. (You can find these notes on the diagram of a piano keyboard on Page

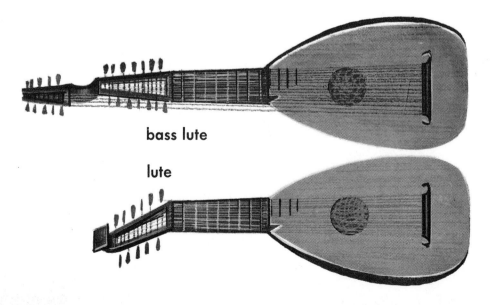

bass lute

lute

22.) The guitar is fretted like the lute and is fingered and plucked in the same way.

Of all the guitars that exist today the classical guitar is most like the earlier instruments. It has a flat neck, which is wide enough so that the distance between the strings is right for quick fingering. The classical guitar has a light construction, which improves the tone. Gut or nylon strings are used, and they are plucked by the thumb and first three fingers of the right hand. Guitars built in the classical form are played in Mexico, Spain, and South America.

The classical guitar is also used on the

jazz
guitar

concert stage. Andres Segovia, who has given concerts since he was fourteen, has made for the classical guitar a well-deserved place in modern music. He plays the classical lute and guitar music of the old musical masters as well as guitar music especially arranged or written for him by today's composers.

Variations of the classical guitar are used by many folk singers for accompaniment. These are sometimes strung with steel strings instead of nylon or gut strings. Usually only simple chords are played as a background for the voice.

Another guitar used today is the jazz guitar of modern instrumental groups. This guitar has a thinner neck, which is slightly rounded. It is strung with steel strings and is played with a plastic pick called a plectrum.

However, the original stringed instru-

30

mandolin

ment of the jazz bands was not the guitar but the banjo. The long fretted neck of the banjo is fastened to a circle of wood covered on one side with a tightly stretched animal skin and open at the back. The bridge across which the strings pass rests on the stretched skin. This unique sounding surface gives the banjo its loud twangy sound. The instrument is strung with from four to nine strings and is tuned in a number of different ways.

Another instrument of the guitar family, which looks like a small lute, is the mandolin. It has the same pear-shaped sound box and has eight strings, which are strung in pairs. Each pair is tuned in unison. The eight strings produce the same notes as those of the violin: G^1, d, a, and e^1. The mandolin is fretted and is played with a plectrum like the jazz guitar. A fast back-and-forth movement of the

banjo

31

plectrum on the double strings gives the mandolin its haunting sound.

A popular variation of the guitar is the ukulele, which is nothing more than a little guitar. It originated in Portugal, traveled to Hawaii, and from there was brought to America. The ukulele comes in two sizes. The larger, called a baritone uke, is still much smaller than a guitar. Its four gut or nylon strings are tuned to the tones of the top four strings of the guitar. The strings of the smaller, or soprano ukulele, are tuned to the notes: a, d, f#, and b.

The ukulele is easy to play and is often used to supply a background of chords for singing. It is usually played with a felt plectrum and is seldom used as a melody instrument. The ukulele is a good instrument to play for fun, and the ukulele fingerings can be helpful in learning to play the guitar.

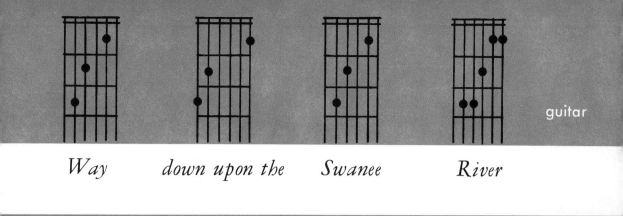

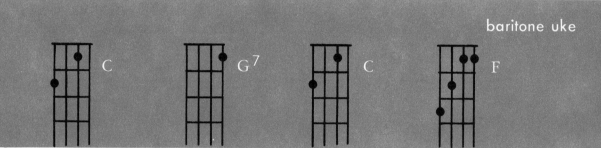

Way   down upon the   Swanee   River

Guitar and uke chord diagrams show the strings
and first few frets of the instruments.
Dots show positions of the fingers on the strings.

Building a Banjo

You can build a simple banjo using a
yardstick, an empty cereal carton, a short
stub of a pencil, and some of the nylon
leader material.

Make two slits on opposite sides of the

carton about ½ inch from the bottom, so that the yardstick can be pushed through, as shown in the drawing. With your coping saw, make a slot in the yardstick half way through at the 1-inch mark. Make a shallow slit at the other end of the yardstick too.

Cut off a piece of nylon line about 45 inches long. Slide it into the notch at the 35-inch mark and tie a loop around the stick to anchor the line. Stretch the line across the bottom of the carton to the opposite end of the yardstick. Tie a loop in the other end of the line, so that the tip of the loop is about ½ inch short of the end of the yardstick. Make the knot tight so that it will not slip. Now stretch the string and push the loop over the end of the yardstick until it catches in the slot

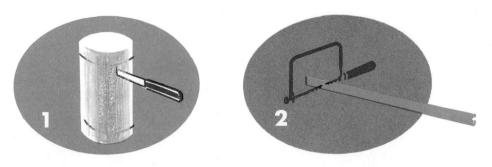

you have made there. The line should now be fairly tight. Slide the carton down to the position shown in the drawing.

Saw off a piece of pencil about 1 ½ inches long or find a stub about that length. Slip this beneath the string, so that it presses against the bottom of the carton. The pencil stub forms a bridge for the string to cross and will transmit the vibrations of the string to the bottom of the carton and to the air inside the carton.

Pluck the string and you will find that it makes a surprisingly loud tone. Try pressing the string against the yardstick at different positions with the fingers of your left hand, as you pluck the string with the thumb of your right hand. Shortening the string raises the pitch. You may be able to play a simple tune by experimenting

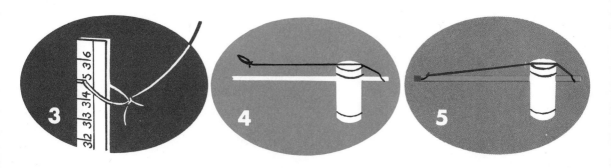

and using the inch markings to identify various notes.

Now you are ready to add frets. Seven rubber bands will provide enough frets so that you can play all of the steps of a major scale. Remove the loop of line from the zero end of the yardstick. Double each rubber band and slip it onto the yardstick, so that it is tightly stretched around the stick. Now replace the loop of line. Place the rubber bands at the inch marks shown in the drawing, and the frets will be tuned to the sol-fa syllables of a major scale. Be sure, however, that the measurements and position of the carton and pencil follow those shown in the drawing. To use a fret as a bridge, push the string against the yardstick just above the fret.

completed banjo

Bowed Stringed Instruments

ravanastron bow

Just as the harp can be traced back to the hunter's bow, so can the bow used with the bowed stringed instruments.

One of the earliest bowed instruments was the ravanastron, used in India about 5000 years ago. In some parts of India it is still used today. The instrument is made of a hollowed-out cylinder of sycamore wood. A narrow stick passes through the sides of the cylinder. Two strings pass over one end of the wooden cylinder and are attached to two wooden pegs, which pass through the narrow neck. The instrument is held straight up and down by the player, who sits on the ground. The strings are bowed with a curved stick strung with silk.

The tones of stringed instruments that

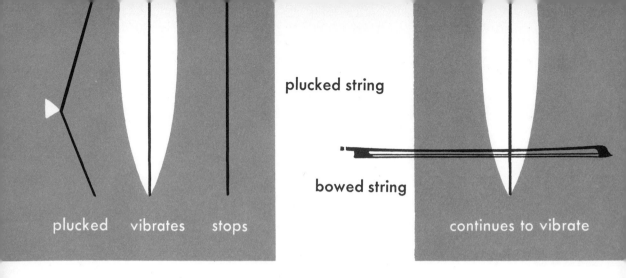

plucked string

bowed string

plucked   vibrates   stops   continues to vibrate

are struck or plucked are sharp and quickly die away. However, when a bow is drawn across a string, the string continues to vibrate and the tone is long and smooth. This difference sets the bowed instruments apart from all the rest of the stringed instruments.

A bowed stringed instrument called the viola da gamba was the most important of its kind for over 200 years. The name meant leg viol, and it covered a family of instruments of different sizes. All of them were played by a player in a seated position. The neck projected upward and the sound box was clamped between the

viola da gamba

knees. The viols had frets of gut, which were tied around the neck like those of the lute. Their six strings were also tuned like the six strings of the lute. Of course, the whole group of strings might be tuned higher or lower, depending on the size of the particular viol.

When the viola da gamba was most popular, the violin was being developed. Eventually it replaced the viola da gamba. The instruments in the violin family had thinner necks than the viola da gambas and they had no frets. The openings in their sound boxes were shaped like an *f* instead of a *c.* Violins had only four strings and they were stretched tighter than those of the viols. The lack of frets around the neck made the new instruments more difficult to finger, and the violinist had to learn by experience where to place his fingers to produce the exact tones desired.

The town of Cremona, in Italy, became famous for its fine violinmakers. Whole families made violins there. One famous violinmaking family was that of Amati. Andreas Amati built the older viols as well as the new violins. His sons continued to build and improve the violin, and his grandson, Nicolo Amati, became the most skillful of the entire family.

One of Nicolo Amati's pupils was Antonio Stradivari, who became perhaps the most famous violinmaker of them all. After learning his trade well, he devoted the later part of his life to giving the violin greater power, so that its tones could fill a large concert hall.

Most violinmakers of the time also made the other instruments similar to the violin. All of the instruments in this family have four strings, *f*-shaped sound openings, indented sides, and fretless necks. They are the foundation of the modern symphony orchestra: first and second violins, violas, cellos, and double basses. The string quartet uses two violins, a viola, and a cello.

The violin has the highest tones in the group. It is tuned to the notes: G^1, d, a, and e^1. Tones are made by pressing a string firmly against the neck of the instrument as it is bowed. It is held so that the sound box is beneath the player's chin.

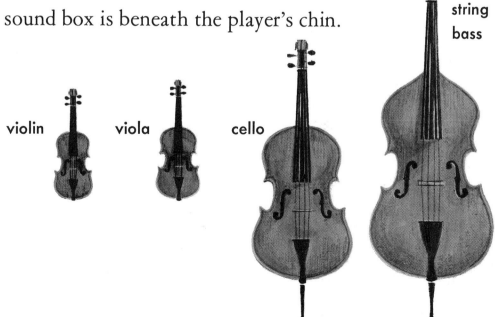

violin   viola   cello   string bass

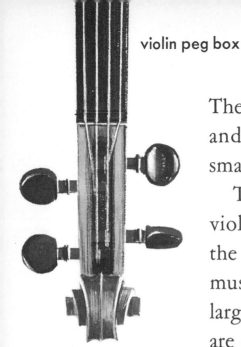

violin peg box

The tones of the violin are rich and bright, and they have surprising power for the small size of the instrument.

The viola is a little larger than the violin, but it is held beneath the chin in the same playing position. A viola player must have strong hands, since the neck is larger than that of a violin and the strings are thicker. The sound of the viola is mellow, almost subdued. Although it can be used as a solo instrument, it is more important as a supporting instrument in a string quartet or an orchestra. It is tuned

string quartet

lower than the violin, to the notes: C^1, G^1, d, and a.

The next largest instrument in this family is the violoncello. The name has now been shortened to cello. It is tuned an octave below the viola to the same notes. It is played in a vertical position, resting on an end pin projecting from the sound box. The sound box is clamped between the knees of the player while the neck rises along his left shoulder.

The double bass, sometimes called the string bass, is the largest of the violin family and looks most like the older viols. It is tuned to the notes: E^3, A^3, D^2, and G^2. Like the cello, it rests on the ground in a vertical position, and the neck extends along the left shoulder of the player. It is so big that the player must stand up or sit on a high stool. As the large orchestra developed, the double bass became the foundation of its tone and rhythm.

bow
hairs

screw

modern violin bow

As bowed stringed instruments changed, so did the bows used to play them. The earliest bows were still very much like the shape of the hunter's bow. A bundle of horsehair was fastened between the ends of a curved stick. By the time of the viols a device had been added to the bow that tightened or loosened the bow hairs, and the stick was straight instead of curved. Still, the more powerful instruments of the violin family required stronger bows. Fifty years after the death of Stradivari, one man turned all of his efforts to improving the violin bow. This man, François Tourte, is sometimes called the Stradivari of the bow.

Tourte developed a method of heating a straight stick of wood and forcing it into a slight curve while it was hot. With proper heating, the wood would hold the curve permanently, and the bow had great strength, because the grain of the wood

44

ran through the curve's entire length.

Tourte curved his bows backward and added a metal clamp that spread the horsehair in a flat ribbon instead of a bundle. The backward curve allowed the violinist to use strong strokes on the strings without bending the stick. Tourte also made many experiments to determine the best length for the bow, the distance the bow hairs should be from the curved stick, and the best weight and balance for the bow. Tourte bows soon became famous, and the form of the violin bow used today still follows that developed by François Tourte.

Building a Bow

You can discover the contrast between the sounds of bowing and plucking by making a bow to use with the banjolike instrument you built from a yardstick and a cereal carton. You will need a coat hanger and about two yards of wool yarn.

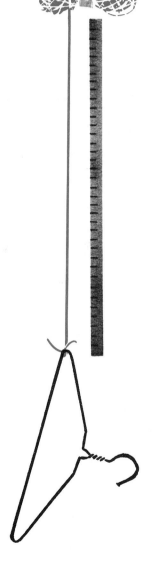

45

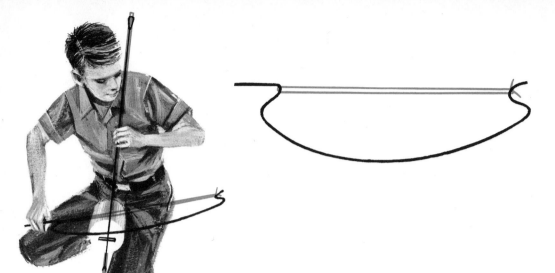

With a pair of pliers, twist off the hook of the coat hanger. Bend the remaining wire into the shape shown in the drawing. Run a long loop of wool yarn between the bends at the ends of the coat hanger, and tie it so that the double strand of yarn is straight and tight.

To bow your instrument, hold it in the up and down playing position of the Indian ravanastron. Let the strands of wool yarn brush along the upper edge of the cereal carton as you draw the bow lightly across the string. You will need some practice before you will get good tones. Try fingering the frets as you bow the string.

By pushing all of the rubber bands down the yardstick toward the carton, you can also try fingering the instrument without frets.

The bow, banjo, monochord, and harp you have built are temporary instruments. While they may have been fun to build and play, only the real stringed instruments will give you long-lasting musical enjoyment. They are well worth the time spent learning to play them.

In the ten thousand years, or longer time, since the hunter first listened to the sound of his bowstring, an almost endless variety of stringed musical instruments has been created. All of them, from the first one-string sound makers to the modern instruments, are based on the same idea. Whether they are plucked, struck, or bowed, each of them depends on the singing tone of a stretched string.

47

Musical Terms

melody tune

accompaniment musical background for the melody

solo instrument or voice with accompaniment or alone

soprano highest range of voice

baritone range between bass and tenor.

bass lowest range of a man's voice

note sign indicating fixed pitch of a tone and its duration

chord two or more notes sounded together

unison instruments (or voices) sounding the same note

half step smallest standard interval between notes (Black and white keys next to each other on a piano are half steps.)

whole step two half steps

octave interval of 12 half steps separating two notes with the same name

sharp sign before a note meaning to raise it one half step

flat sign before a note meaning to lower it one half step

sol-fa syllables do, re, mi, fa, sol, la, ti, do (tones sounded by C D E F G A B C on the piano)

scale a series of successive tones starting and ending with *do*

key name of the basic scale on which a tune is built

vibration fast, regular, back-and-forth movement

amplify to increase, to make louder

48